ALL ABOUT FALL

Leaves in Fall

by Martha E. H. Rustad

Consulting Editor: Gail Saunders-Smith, PhD

Capstone
Press

Mankato, Minnesota

Pebble Plus is published by Capstone Press,
151 Good Counsel Drive, P.O. Box 669, Mankato, Minnesota 56002.
www.capstonepress.com

1 2 3 4 5 6 12 11 10 09 08 07

Library of Congress Cataloging-in-Publication Data
Rustad, Martha E. H. (Martha Elizabeth Hillman), 1975–
    Leaves in fall / by Martha E. H. Rustad.
    p. cm. — (Pebble Plus. All about fall)
    Summary: "Simple text and photographs present leaves in fall"—Provided by publisher.
    Includes bibliographical references and index.
    ISBN-13: 978-1-4296-0024-8 (hardcover)
    ISBN-10: 1-4296-0024-1 (hardcover)
    1. Leaves—Juvenile literature. 2. Fall foliage—Juvenile literature. I. Title. II. Series.
QK649.R88 2008
578.4'3—dc22   2006102054

Editorial Credits
Sarah L. Schuette, editor; Veronica Bianchini, designer

Photo Credits
Capstone Press/Karon Dubke, all

Pebble Plus thanks the Minnesota Landscape Arboretum in Chaska, Minnesota, for the use of their location
    during photo shoots.

Note to Parents and Teachers

The All about Fall set supports national science standards related to changes during
the seasons. This book describes and illustrates leaves in fall. The images support early
readers in understanding the text. The repetition of words and phrases helps early
readers learn new words. This book also introduces early readers to subject-specific
vocabulary words, which are defined in the Glossary section. Early readers may need
assistance to read some words and to use the Table of Contents, Glossary, Read More,
Internet Sites, and Index sections of the book.

Table of Contents

Fall Is Here

Summer is over. It's fall.

Leaves start to change color.

Colorful Trees

Broad maple leaves become red, orange, and yellow.

Oak leaves

turn red and brown.

9

Round gingko leaves

change to yellow.

Evergreen needles do not change color.

They stay green all year.

13

Falling Leaves

The weather gets colder.

The days are shorter.

Leaves turn brown and die.

14

Leaves float to the ground.

They crunch under your feet.

People rake leaves in fall.

You can play in the piles.

A New Season

The trees are bare.

Winter is here.

A new season begins.

Glossary

bare—not covered or empty; trees look bare when the leaves fall off.

broad—wide; maple leaves are broad with pointed edges.

crunch—to make a loud noise when crushed

evergreen—a tree that has green leaves all year

needle—a thin, pointed leaf on an evergreen tree

season—one of the four parts of the year; the seasons are spring, summer, fall, and winter.

Read More

DeGezelle, Terri. *Autumn.* Bridgestone Books: Seasons. Mankato, Minn.: Capstone Press, 2003.

Parker, Victoria. *Fall.* Raintree Sprouts: Days In. Chicago: Raintree, 2005.

Schuette, Sarah L. *Let's Look at Fall.* Pebble Plus: Investigate the Seasons. Mankato, Minn.: Capstone Press, 2007.

Internet Sites

FactHound offers a safe, fun way to find Internet sites related to this book. All of the sites on FactHound have been researched by our staff.

Here's how:

1. Visit *www.facthound.com*

2. Choose your grade level.

3. Type in this book ID **1429600241** for age-appropriate sites. You may also browse subjects by clicking on letters, or by clicking on pictures and words.

4. Click on the **Fetch It** button.

FactHound will fetch the best sites for you!

Index

Word Count: 86
Grade: 1
Early-Intervention Level: 12